Making Sense of Maths

All things equal

Paul Dickinson
Stella Dudzic
Frank Eade
Steve Gough
Sue Hough

HODDER
EDUCATION

The publishers would like to thank the following for permission to reproduce copyright material:

Photo credits: page 7 *all photos* © Sue Hough; page 9 *all photos* © Sue Hough; page 10 *b* © Sue Hough; page 14 *all photos* © Sue Hough; pages 33–39 *all photos* © Kate Crossland-Page; page 41 *all photos* © Kate Crossland-Page; page 45 *all photos* © Kate Crossland-Page; pages 50–51 *all photos* © Kate Crossland-Page

t = top, *c* = centre, *b* = bottom, *l* = left, *r* = right

All designated trademarks and brands are protected by their respective trademarks.

Every effort has been made to trace all copyright holders, but if any have been inadvertently overlooked, the Publishers will be pleased to make the necessary arrangements at the first opportunity.

Although every effort has been made to ensure that website addresses are correct at time of going to press, Hodder Education cannot be held responsible for the content of any website mentioned in this book. It is sometimes possible to find a relocated web page by typing in the address of the home page for a website in the URL window of your browser.

Hachette UK's policy is to use papers that are natural, renewable and recyclable products and made from wood grown in sustainable forests. The logging and manufacturing processes are expected to conform to the environmental regulations of the country of origin.

Orders: please contact Bookpoint Ltd, 130 Milton Park, Abingdon, Oxon OX14 4SB. Telephone: (44) 01235 827720. Fax: (44) 01235 400454. Lines are open 9.00–5.00, Monday to Saturday, with a 24-hour message answering service. Visit our website at www.hoddereducation.co.uk

© Paul Dickinson, Stella Dudzic, Frank Eade, Steve Gough, Sue Hough 2012

First published in 2012 by
Hodder Education, an Hachette UK company,
338 Euston Road
London NW1 3BH

Impression number 5 4 3 2 1
Year 2016 2015 2014 2013 2012

Cover photo © Sue Hough
Illustrations by Pantek Media, Maidstone, Kent
Typeset in ITC Stone Informal by Pantek Media, Maidstone, Kent
Printed in Spain

A catalogue record for this title is available from the British Library

ISBN 978 1444 169126

Contents

Chapter 5: Seeing it differently

Introduction

These books are intended to help you to make sense of the maths you do in school and the maths you need to use outside school. They have already been tried out in classrooms, and are the result of many comments made by the teachers and the students who have used them. Students told us that after working with these materials they were more able to understand the maths they had done, and teachers found that students also did better in tests and examinations.

Most of the time you will be working 'in context' – in other words, in real-life situations that you will either have been in yourself or can imagine being in. For example, in this book you will be looking at ways of recording orders at a chip shop, solving problems with weighing scales and using number lines for solving equations.

You will regularly be asked to 'draw something' – drawings and sketches are very important in maths and often help us to solve problems and to see connections between different topics. In the trials, students found that drawing a weighing scales picture or a number line diagram helped them to develop an understanding of how to solve an equation.

You will also be expected to talk about your maths, explaining your ideas to small groups or to the whole class. We all learn by explaining our own ideas and by listening to and trying out the ideas of others.

Finally, of course, you will be expected to practice solving problems and answering examination questions.

We hope that through working in this way you will come to understand the maths you do, enjoy examination success, and be confident when using your maths outside school.

Taking orders

1 Jane works at a chip shop at weekends. The price list is shown here.

Fish	£2.60
Sausage	£1.20
Chips	£1.10
Peas	£0.50
Gravy	£0.40

Sometimes when people come in with an order they ask for things like, 'Fish and chips three times please.'

What would be the price of this order? Write down the calculations that you did to work it out.

2 Jane has to work out the price as quickly as possible, so she talks to Azim who also works at the shop. Below is the conversation they had about working out the cost of the order.

I do the price of 1 fish and 1 lot of chips, then times that by 3.

I do the price of 3 fish, then the price of 3 lots of chips and add them up.

Do both of these give the same cost for the full order?

3 Use Jane's method to work out the cost of the following orders:
   a) Fish and chips twice and an extra portion of chips.
   b) Sausage and chips three times and two portions of peas.

4 Use Azim's method to work out the following orders:
   a) Fish, chips and peas twice.
   b) Sausage and chips four times and one portion of peas.

5 At lunchtime, people sometimes come in with big orders. Why do you think this is?

6 One lunchtime, a full order is fish and chips three times, sausage and chips twice, fish and peas twice, and two extra portions of chips.

Fish	£2.60
Sausage	£1.20
Chips	£1.10
Peas	£0.50
Gravy	£0.40

What is the full cost of this order? Show carefully the calculations you did to work it out and discuss these with someone in your class.

7 If an order is very long, or if it is ordered over the phone, the person taking the order writes it down first and then works out the cost. They use '*f*' for the cost of fish, and so on.

Azim writes down an order as:

$$3(f + c) + 4(s + p) + 1c + 2p + 2(f + p)$$

Jane works out the cost by writing down:

$$5f + 4s + 4c + 8p$$

Will this give the right answer? Explain why or why not.

8 Work out the full cost of this order.

9 The following orders have all been written down by Azim. For each order, write it out in full as Jane would do, but make it as simple as possible. (You do not have to work out the cost of each one.)

a) $2(s + c) + 3(f + p) + 3(f + c) + 2p + 3c + 2s$

b) $2(f + c + g) + 2(f + c) + f + 3(s + c + p) + (s + c) + 2(c + g) + 3c$

c) $5(s + c + g) + (f + c) + 2(f + c + p + g) + 3(f + c + g) + 2s + 2c$

10 Jane wrote down an order as $10f + 6c$. One possibility is that this was originally ordered over the phone as 'fish and chips twice, eight more fish, and four more lots of chips'.

Write down two more possible ways in which this order might have been given over the phone.

11 Below are three more orders that Jane wrote down. In each case, give two possible ways in which they might have been ordered over the phone.

a) $8s + 5c$

b) $12f + 16c$

c) $6f + 3c + 3g$

12 Later, Jane gave the following order to Azim: $6s + 4c$.

To work out the cost, Azim wrote this as $4(s + c) + 2s$.

Without working out the cost, decide whether Azim is right to do this and explain your answer.

13 Paul, who also works at the chip shop, suggested that it would have been even easier to work out the cost if it had been written as $2(3s + 2c)$.

Do you agree with Paul? Explain your answer.

14 Another order of Jane's was: $6c + 9s + 3g$.

Azim wrote: $6(s + c) + 3s + 3g$.

Paul wrote: $3(3s + 2c + g)$.

Jane said: 'You could also have written it as $6(s + c) + 3(s + g)$.'

Explain carefully why all of these are really the same order.

15 Write down how you think Azim or Paul would write the following orders of Jane's. You don't have to work out the cost, but try to write each order as simply as possible. You might like to write down a couple of different possibilities as we did above.

a) $3s + 3c$

b) $4f + 2c + 2p$

c) $2c + 4s + 6f$

d) $3s + 3f + 6p + 9c$

e) $12s + 9c$

f) $12f + 8c + 4g$

Summary

In this chapter you have seen how orders at a chip shop can be written in different ways. For example, one person wrote an order as:

$$2(s + c) + 3(f + p) + 3(f + c) + 2p + 3c + 2s$$

This could also be written as:

$$4s + 8c + 6f + 5p$$

Or as:

$$4(s + 2c) + 5(f + p) + f$$

These are all equivalent expressions for this order.

The see-saw

1 **a)** What happens when an adult goes on one side of a see-saw with a toddler on the other side?

   b) Look at the family shown below. What combinations of people would you suggest should go on the see-saw together?

The human balance

1 Work in pairs. Person 1 stands with their arms outstretched to make a human balance. Person 2 places objects on the palms of Person 1's hands. Person 1 then has to tilt to show which object they think is heavier. Repeat with different objects and take it in turns to be the human balance.

2 Direct your teacher to make a human balance with five marker pens on each palm. Students take it in turns to remove or add marker pens. After each move the teacher has to tilt to show what has happened to the scales.

The grocer

2 Here is a set of weighing scales.

There is nothing in the dish and there are no weights on the other side.

How can you tell that these scales are balanced?

3 **a)** Look closely at these photographs and describe what you see.

16 oz   8 oz   2 oz   1 oz $\frac{1}{2}$ oz $\frac{1}{4}$ oz

b) How much flour is in the bag?

4 The weighing scales in the pictures date back to 1895. In those days people used to go to the grocer's to buy food such as flour, rice, sugar, and so on. It was not available in pre-packed quantities as it is today. Nor were there digitalised weighing scales as we see in supermarkets today.

The customer would ask the grocer for a certain amount of an ingredient.

The grocer would place 10 oz in weights on the scales. They would then begin to spoon flour onto the tray side of the scales. When the scales balanced this would tell the grocer that they had the required quantity of flour.

Each set of scales came with a standard set of seven weights. These were:

$\frac{1}{4}$ oz $\frac{1}{2}$ oz   1 oz   2 oz

4 oz   8 oz   16 oz (= 1 pound)

The set of weighing scales shown in the photo above has one of the original weights missing.

Write down a statement about the weight of flour in each of the following pictures.

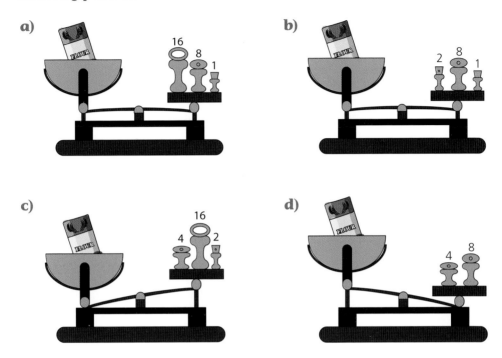

a)

b)

c)

d)

5 What is the largest quantity you could measure using the standard set of seven weights?

 Now do Workbook exercise 2.1 on pages 1–2 of your workbook.

Missing weights

6 It is possible to buy antique sets of these weighing scales at auctions and online. As you might expect, the set of weights is not always complete.

Elaine purchases scales that only have the following weights:

1 oz   2 oz   4 oz   16 oz

She starts to make a list of the quantities she will and won't be able to measure.

Elaine's Grandma thinks she has made a mistake with her list. See if you can find it.

$$1\,oz = 1\,oz \checkmark$$

$$2\,oz = 2\,oz \checkmark$$

$$3\,oz = 1 + 2\,oz \checkmark$$

$$4\,oz = 4\,oz \checkmark$$

$$5\,oz = 4 + 1\,oz$$

$$6\,oz = 4 + 2\,oz$$

$$7\,oz = 4 + 2 + 1\,oz$$

8 oz   can't do

9 oz   can't do

7 Elaine's Grandma says she knows how to measure 10 oz as well, and she draws the following picture:

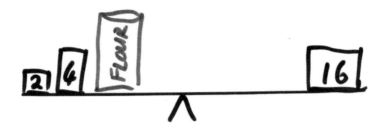

Explain how you know this flour weighs 10 oz.

 Turn to pages 3–4 of your workbook and do Workbook exercise 2.2.

 Now do Workbook exercise 2.3 on pages 5–6 of your workbook.

8 Make up four weighing pictures like the ones in **Workbook exercise 2.3**. Work out your answers, and then give the problems to your neighbour to solve.

9 a) Compare the answers you found for each other's problems.

b) How realistic were the problems you designed?

(**Note:** A small banana weighs roughly 4 oz and a supermarket-sized bag of sugar weighs roughly 2 pounds or 32 oz.)

Tipping the balance

 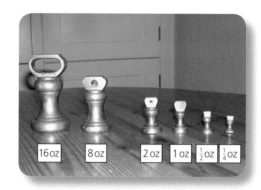

10 Describe what you see in the two pictures below.

11 In the second picture a 1 oz weight has been added to the right-hand side of the scales and this has tipped the balance. Describe some ways in which you could make the scales balance again.

12 **a)** Describe what has happened from one picture to the next.

Peppers

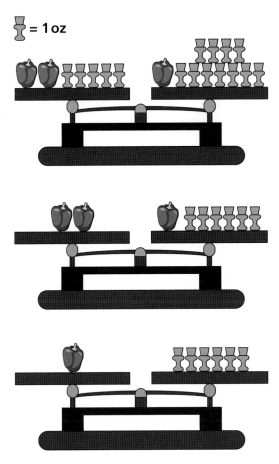

= 1 oz

b) Do you think the scales *would* remain in balance at each stage? Explain your answer.

13 **a)** Draw your own version of the following picture:

Oranges

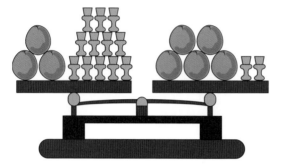

b) Imagine that you are adding or removing objects from the scales shown. Draw the pictures to match your moves.

c) What is the weight of one orange?

14 Two Year 11 students answered **question 13** in quite different ways.

Gary's method:

2 oranges weigh 10 oz

1 orange weighs 5 oz

Ellie's method:

I added weights and oranges to make
the scales exactly the same.
2 oranges added must weigh 10 ounces added.
So one orange weighs 5 ounces.

a) Describe what Gary has done to solve the problem.

b) Describe what Ellie has done to solve the problem.

c) How does Ellie know that 2 oranges must weigh the same as 10 ounces?

d) Which method do you prefer?

Turn to your workbook and do Workbook exercise 2.4 on pages 7–10.

Shorthand for balancing

15 When answering the questions in **Workbook exercise 2.4**, some students started to write a shorthand version of the pictures.

Look at the shorthand they wrote for **questions 1** and **2F** below. Does it make sense to you? Explain what they have done.

A. Bananas

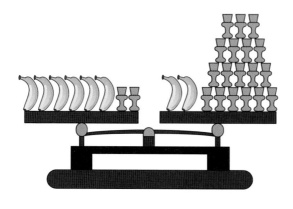

$$6b + 2 = 2b + 18$$

F. Apples

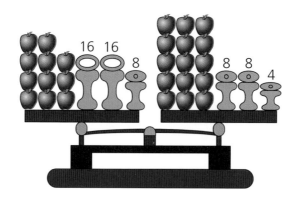

$$11a + 16 + 16 + 8 = 15a + 8 + 8 + 4$$

16 Here is the shorthand for another balance problem:

$$16p + 14 = 10p + 44$$

   a) Draw a scales picture for this problem. Try to do this in more than one way.

   b) Work out the value of p.

   c) What object do you think p could be?

17 **a)** Draw a scales picture for the balance problem:

$$8 + 6q = 20 + 3q$$

   b) Work out the value of q.

   c) Here is a scales picture for the problem:

$$8r + 15 > 5r + 21$$

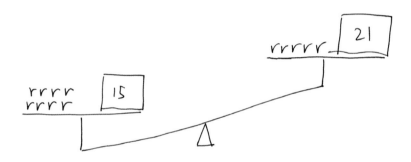

   Does this picture fit with the problem or not? Explain.

   d) Use the picture to find out some information about r.

 Turn to pages 11–12 of your workbook and do Workbook exercise 2.5.

More shorthand

18 Try to make some sense of the shorthand written below by drawing a scales picture.

$$3(a + 2) = a + 12$$

Compare your ideas with the rest of your class.

19 **a)** Draw a scales picture for the balance problem:

$$5b + 7 = 3(b + 4)$$

b) Work out the value of b.

 Turn to pages 13–14 of your workbook and do Workbook exercise 2.6.

Summary

In this chapter you worked on the idea of balanced weighing scales and what this could tell you about the weight of an object. For example:

Bananas

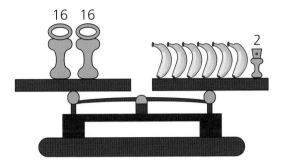

Here you worked out that the weight of a banana must be around 5 ounces, i.e. $b = 5$.

Apples

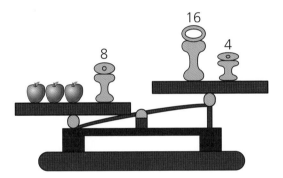

Here you worked out that the weight of an apple must be more than 4 ounces, i.e. $a > 4$.

You developed strategies for solving weighing problems where the objects appeared on both sides of the scales. For example:

Tangerines

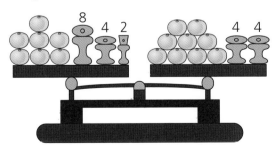

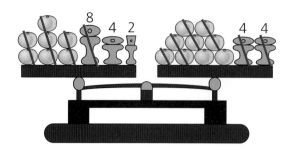

One strategy involved removing objects from the scales.

Then you can figure out what an object weighs from what you have left.

$$6 = 2t$$
$$t = 3$$

You developed ways of solving balance problems by drawing scales pictures.

For example, the problem $12y + 4 = 7y + 14$ can be drawn as:

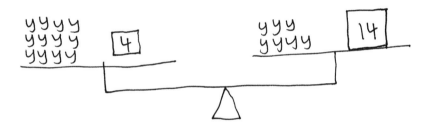

By removing objects from both sides of the scales:

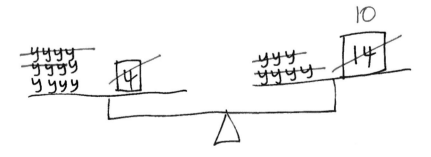

You can see that:

$$5y = 10$$
$$y = 2$$

Froggit!

1 Freddie (the frog) and his friends like to play a game that involves getting from one point to another in a number of equal jumps.

So, for example, Freddie covers a distance of 9 m in three equal jumps.

What was the length of each of Freddie's jumps?

2 Tina isn't as good at the game as Freddie. She makes four equal jumps but is still a metre short.

How far was each of Tina's jumps?

3 The smaller frogs now join in as well, but obviously using much shorter distances. The table below shows what happened. Freddie and Tina are already in the table, so you can check your answers to **questions 1** and **2**.

Copy the table and fill in the blanks.

Frog	Total distance to jump	Number of equal-sized jumps	Finishing point	Size of each jump
Freddie	9 m	3	Exactly right	3 m
Tina	9 m	4	1 m short	2 m
Tommy	30 cm	7	2 cm short	
Funky	27 cm	5	3 cm too far	
Tillie		5	2 cm too far	10 cm

4 Steve is a frogologist at a university. He watches the frogs and estimates the distances that they are jumping. Instead of using a table, Steve writes down his observations and then draws a diagram for each frog.

So, for Freddie he writes down $3x = 9$ and then draws:

Freddie

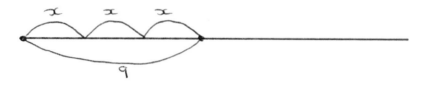

For Tina he writes $4x + 1 = 9$ and then draws:

Tina

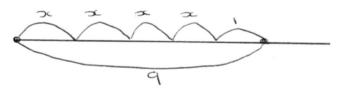

The writing and part of his drawings for Tommy and Funky are shown below. Copy the diagrams, label them, and add any missing information.

Tommy

$7x + 2 = 30$

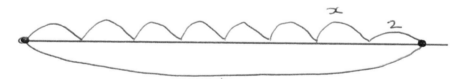

Funky

$5x - 3 = 27$

5 When Steve gets back to the university, he looks at five other drawings that he did last week.

For each of these drawings, describe what each frog did. Then write down the size of each equal jump.

a)

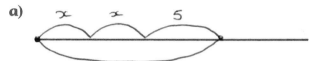

b)

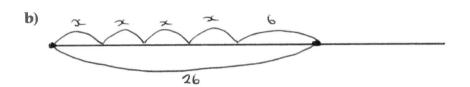

c)

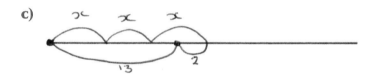

d)

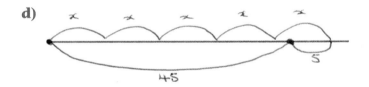

e)

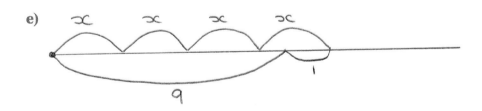

6 Steve also has some results where he wrote down what happened, but hasn't yet done the drawings. Make a number line drawing for each of the following:

a) $3x + 2 = 11$

b) $15 = 4x + 3$

c) $27 = 5x - 3$

d) $6x - 4 = 32$

Equations on a number line

7 While Steve is on holiday, Simon records the frogs' jumps for him. Unfortunately he does it in a different way, and doesn't write down the total distance. Instead he draws the following:

And he writes: $3x + 14 = 5x + 6$.

When Steve asks Simon what the drawing means, he says:

> The frog was trying to get from point A to point B. First it tried 3 equal jumps but was 14 short; next it tried 5 equal jumps and was 6 short. You can still work out the size of each equal jump.

Explain carefully how Simon can still work out the size of each equal jump.

8 In school, a teacher uses some of Steve's drawings to play the game 'Say what you can see'.

For $3x + 14 = 5x + 6$ he uses:

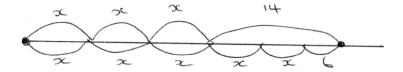

Some ideas from the class were:

$2x + 14 = 4x + 6$

$3x = 3x$

$2x + 6 = 14$

$3x + 14 - 6 = 5x$

$3x + 14 - 6 - 5x = 0$

$5x + 6 - 14 - 2x = x$

Discuss the above statements with your class. Write down two more statements that you could make from looking at the number line.

9 Beth was trying to write down some statements for the equation: $4x + 5 = x + 12$.

She wrote the following:

a) $4x = 12$

b) $4x = x + 7$

c) $3x + 5 = 12$

d) $5x + 5 = 2x + 12$

e) $4x + 5 + 12 = x$

f) $8x + 10 = 2x + 24$

g) $4x + 5 - 12 - x = 0$

Some of her statements are **correct** and some are **incorrect**. For each statement, say whether it is right or not and give a reason. For the incorrect ones, you might be able to say why she has made the mistake and what the correct answer should be.

10 In each of the following, one statement has been done for you. Copy the drawing and then write down three other statements you could make by looking at the number line.

a)

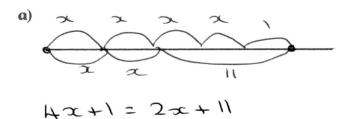

$$4x+1 = 2x+11$$

b)

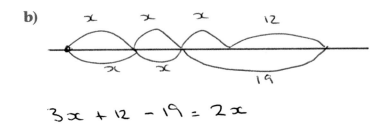

$$3x + 12 - 19 = 2x$$

c)

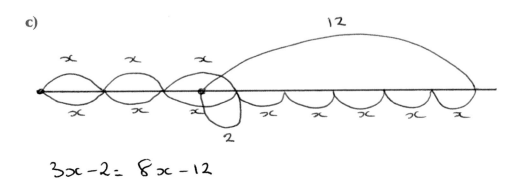

$$3x - 2 = 8x - 12$$

11 Use your statements to work out the value of x for each part of **question 10**.

Now do Workbook exercise 3.1 on pages 15–18 of your workbook.

12 Make a number line drawing for the following statements and then try to work out the value of x, showing carefully how you got your answer.

    a) $5x + 3 = 18$

    b) $3x + 14 = 5x + 5$

    c) $5x - 3 = 2x + 7$

    d) $4x - 5 = 6x - 10$

    e) $7 - x = 3$

    f) $10 - 2x = x + 1$

13 In spring, the frogs jump around all day and there are some serious numbers involved! For one set of jumps, Steve wrote down:

$48x + 24 = 27x + 87$

Steve originally drew this as:

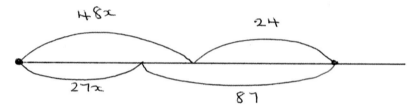

But then he re-drew it as:

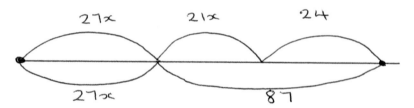

Why do you think Steve re-drew it in this way?

14 Work out the value of x, explaining carefully how you did it.

15 Make a number line drawing for the following, and then work out the value of x in each case.

    a) $17x + 42 = 27x + 12$

    b) $35x + 9 = 20x + 54$

    c) $32x - 8 = 14x + 82$

    d) $15 - 8x = 22 - 10x$

    e) $12x - 3 = 31 - 5x$

 Now do Workbook exercise 3.2 on pages 19–20 of your workbook.

Brackets on a number line

16 John is trying to answer the following GCSE question:

Solve the equation $3(x + 2) + 1 = 2(2x + 1) + 3$

The teacher suggests that John draws this on a number line, so he draws:

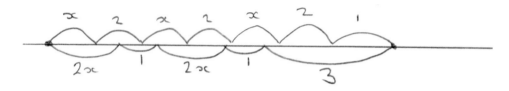

Is this correct? Give a reason for your answer.

17 Carol is also doing this question. She suggests to John that it would be better if he now reorganised his line so that it looks like this:

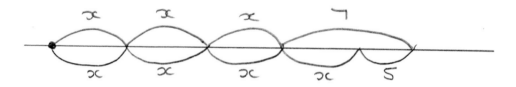

a) Is Carol's drawing equivalent to John's?

b) Why do you think Carol reorganised her number line?

c) Use Carol's line to work out the value of x, explaining carefully how you got your answer.

18 For the following questions, first draw a number line as John did. Then reorganise the number line in the same way that Carol did. Finally, solve the equation to find the value of x.

a) $2(x + 3) = 15$

b) $2(x + 5) + 7 = 3(2x + 3)$

c) $4(2x + 3) = 2(3x + 10)$

d) $3(x + 1) + 7 = 2(4x + 1) + 3$

19 John likes Carol's method, so tries to write the equation in her way straight away. For $4(x + 5) = 3(2x + 2)$ he draws:

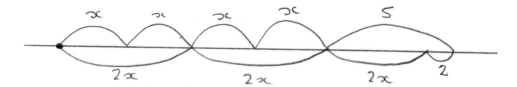

John's drawing is **not correct**. He has made a mistake that many people make when working with brackets.

a) Explain carefully what John has done wrong and why you think he made this mistake.

b) Do a correct drawing for this equation and use it to work out the value of x.

Student's Book exercise 3.1

Use Carol's method to solve the following equations.

1 $2(x + 3) = 14$

2 $3(2x + 3) = 2(2x + 5)$

3 $3(2x - 1) = 21$

4 $3(x + 6) + 4 = 5(2x + 1) + 3$

5 $5x + 13 = 7(x - 1)$

Summary

In this section you have used a number line to picture equations and to find the value of the unknown quantity.

For example, for the equation $3x + 14 = 5x + 6$ we can picture a journey of length $3x + 14$ being the same length as a journey of $5x + 6$. We can then draw:

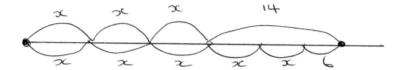

We can then write down other journeys. For example:

$3x + 14 - 6 = 5x$

We can also see that $2x + 6 = 14$ and that $2x = 8$.

From this we can then see that each 'x jump' must be a length of 4.

So $x = 4$.

You have also seen how a number line can help to picture and solve equations that have brackets in them.

For example, the equation $3(x + 2) + 1 = 2(2x + 1) + 3$ can firstly be drawn as:

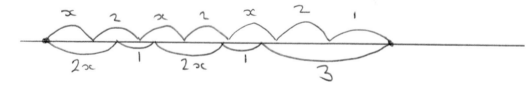

And then rearranged as:

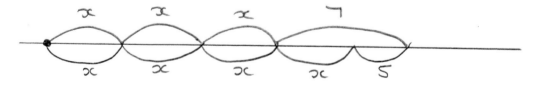

From this, we can see that $x = 2$.

Frogs and scales together

1 Matt and Louise are discussing their answers to **question 9** on page 27.

The starting equation was:

$4x + 5 = x + 12$

Matt drew:

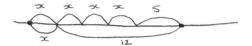

Part **c)** of **question 9** asked if $3x + 5 = 12$ was also true. Matt said:

> This is true. I just take *x* off each journey, so top and bottom will still be the same length.

He drew:

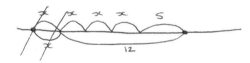

Matt also thought that part **b)** of **question 9** was true.

He wrote $4x = x + 7$ and said:

> This is true because …

Write down how Matt would have explained his answer and make a drawing to show this.

2 When Louise does $4x + 5 = x + 12$, she prefers to see it as a balance and draws:

For $3x + 5 = 12$, she then says:

The scales will still balance because I have just taken an x weight from each scale.

She draws:

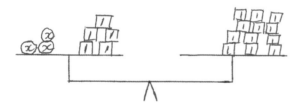

How would Louise explain that $4x = x + 7$ also keeps the scales in balance?

Draw the scales to show this.

3 If $4x + 5 = x + 12$, then it is also true that $5x + 5 = 2x + 12$.

How would both Matt and Louise explain why this must be true?

④ Sean thinks that part **e)** of **question 9** is also correct.

That is, if $4x + 5 = x + 12$, then it is also true that $4x + 5 + 12 = x$.

Use either Matt's or Louise's method, and a drawing, to explain why Sean is wrong.

⑤ If $4x + 5 = x + 12$, must it be true that $8x + 10 = 2x + 24$?

Use either Matt's or Louise's method to explain your answer.

⑥ Matt says:

> I always see an equation as 2 equal journeys on a line. So if I add the same distance to each journey, they will still be equal. I can also take the same amount off each journey, or even times or divide each journey by the same amount. Sometimes I don't even draw a line, I just do:

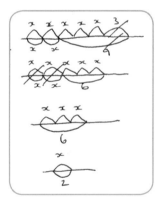

$$5x + 3 = 2x + 9$$

$$5x \quad = 2x + 6 \qquad \text{Take 3 from both journeys}$$

$$3x \quad = 6 \qquad \text{Take } 2x \text{ from both journeys}$$

$$x \quad = 2$$

Show how Matt would solve the equation $4x + 1 = 2x + 11$. It is up to you whether or not you draw the number line.

7 Louise says:

I always see an equation as 2 equal scales so they balance. So if I add the same amount to each scale, they will still balance. I can also take the same amount off each scale, or even times or divide each scale by the same amount. Sometimes I don't draw the scales, I just do:

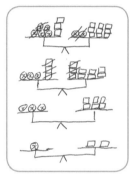

$5x + 3 = 2x + 9$ ⟩ Take $2x$ from both sides

$3x + 3 = 9$ ⟩ Take 3 from both sides

$3x = 6$

$x = 2$

Show how Louise would solve the equation $4x + 1 = 2x + 11$.

8 Although Matt and Louise picture equations in different ways, when they don't do drawings, their work looks exactly the same. Copy and complete the solution below.

$3x + 10 = 7x + 2$ ⟩ Take 2 from both

$3x + 8 = 7x$

9 Do you think the working in **question 8** belongs to Matt or Louise?

10 Matt and Louise are working on another equation, $4x + 15 = 7x - 3$.

Louise says...

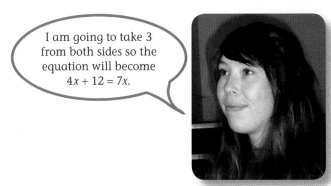

> I am going to take 3 from both sides so the equation will become $4x + 12 = 7x$.

Matt says...

> I don't think that is right. When you draw $4x + 15 = 7x - 3$ you can see that $4x + 12$ is a shorter journey than $7x$.

Matt draws...

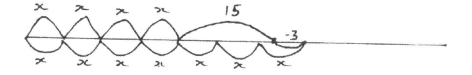

a) How can you tell from the line that $4x + 12$ is not the same as $7x$?

b) By looking at the line, what is $7x$ equal to?

Matt says...

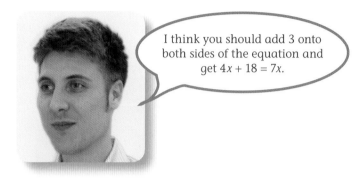

I think you should add 3 onto both sides of the equation and get $4x + 18 = 7x$.

c) Explain using Matt's drawing why $4x + 18 = 7x$ is correct.

d) Complete the solution to $4x + 15 = 7x - 3$.

11 a) If you wanted to solve $2x + 9 = 4x - 5$, what would be the first thing you would do to each side of the equation?

b) Solve $2x + 9 = 4x - 5$

Student's Book exercise 4.1

Solve the following equations, showing clearly what you are doing at each stage:

1 $5x + 3 = 38$

2 $6x + 5 = 2x + 17$

3 $2x + 10 = 4x - 1$

4 $4x - 5 = x + 3$

5 $9 - 4x = x - 6$

---

12 Matt and Louise are struggling with $15 - 8x = 22 - 10x$.

Salman says:

> I don't like negatives, so I always start by adding enough to each side to get rid of them.

He writes:

$15 - 8x = 22 - 10x$

$15 + 2x = 22$ ⟩ Add 10x to both sides

Why did Salman add $10x$ to both sides and not $8x$?

13 Complete Salman's solution from **question 12** to find x.

14 Solve the equation: $-7 - 3x = 8 - 4x$.

15 Solve the equation: $2x - 6 = x - 9$.

Student's Book exercise 4.2

Solve the following equations.

1 $3x + 4 = 10 - x$ 2 $2n + 5 = 5n - 10$

3 $6p - 8 = 4p - 3$ 4 $12 - 3t = 18 - 5t$

5 $5y + 2 = 3y - 2$ 6 $4x - 3 = x$

7 $7x + 1 = 3x - 11$ 8 $3x - 2 = -5x - 10$

9 $2(2x + 1) = 3(x + 2)$ 10 $5x - 4 = 4(2x + 5)$

Easy to see

So far in this book you have used different methods to solve some quite difficult equations. However, some equations can be solved quickly with a common-sense approach. For example, if $x + 4 = 11$, then it must mean that x is equal to 7 (because $7 + 4 = 11$). When we can **see** the solution quickly like this we say the solution is **EASY TO SEE**.

Student's Book exercise 4.3

The solution to the following equations should be EASY TO SEE. In each case, write down the value of x:

1   $x - 5 = 16$

2   $x + 3 = 15$

3   $4 + x = 45$

4   $8 - x = 6$

5   $10 - x = 12$

6   $2x + 2 = 18$

7   $5 + 3x = 17$

8   $5x - 6 = 44$

9   $\dfrac{x}{2} + 5 = 15$

10 $\dfrac{x}{3} - 6 = 0$

16 As you become more familiar with equations, it's likely that more of them will become EASY TO SEE. For example, Ava says that the solution to the equation $11 - 2x = 5$ is EASY TO SEE. She says:

If 11 take away something is 5, then the something must be 6. So $2x$ equals 6 and so x must be 3.

Marc also thinks that $11 - 2x = 5$ is EASY TO SEE, but he does it a slightly different way.

I cover up the x bit and write down $11 -$ $= 5$. So the covered-up bit must be 6. So $2x$ is 6 and so x is 3.

Marc actually wrote down:

$$11 - \boxed{2x} = 5$$
$$11 - \boxed{6} = 5$$
$$2x = 6$$
$$x = 3$$

Tom joins in and claims that the equation $2(x - 3) = 8$ is also EASY TO SEE. He simply writes down:

$$x - 3 = 4$$
$$\text{so} \quad x = 7$$

Explain carefully how Tom has done this.

Now turn to pages 21–22 in your workbook and complete Workbook exercise 4.1.

17 From the list of equations below, pick out those that you think are EASY TO SEE and solve them. Compare your answers with others in the class.

a) $3x = 24$

b) $2x + 8 = 5x + 2$

c) $4(x + 1) = 32$

d) $\dfrac{x - 5}{6} = 3$

e) $2(x + 7) = 5(x - 1)$

f) $11 - 2x = 5$

g) $6x - 7 = 3x + 11$

h) $3(x^2 + 1) = 30$

i) $2(x - 3) + 4 = 20$

j) $\dfrac{10}{x} = 2$

k) $\dfrac{18}{x} = 3$

l) $6 + 9x = 14 + 5x$

> When an equation is **not** EASY TO SEE, we need a method for solving it. Some students imagine a number line or a pair of scales to help with the algebra.

Trial and improvement

18. If 75 is too big and 25 is too small, what do you know about the size of the number?

19. If 56 is too big and 55 is too small, what do you know about the number?

20. If 30 is too big and 20 is too small, what would be a good number to guess next? Explain your answer.

21 Lottie and Alice are solving equations. They get stuck on $x^3 + x = 50$. Lottie thinks she could guess the answer. Her first guess is $x = 4$.

Do you think $x = 4$ is a good guess? Explain why.

22 Lottie checks her guess by substituting $x = 4$ into $x^3 + x$ and seeing if it is equal to 50.

Try $x = 4$ so:
$$x^3 + x = 4^3 + 4$$
$$= (4 \times 4 \times 4) + 4$$
$$= 64 + 4$$
$$= 68$$

Lottie says 4 is too big, as 68 is bigger than 50.

Lottie now tries $x = 3$:

Try $x = 3$ so:
$$x^3 + x = 3^3 + 3$$
$$= (3 \times 3 \times 3) + 3$$
$$= 27 + 3$$
$$= 30$$

Lottie says 3 is too small, as 30 is smaller than 50.

As $x = 3$ is too small and $x = 4$ is too big, Lottie knows the value for x is between 3 and 4. She tries $x = 3.5$.

Try $x = 3.5$ so:
$$x^3 + x = 3.5^3 + 3.5$$
$$= (3.5 \times 3.5 \times 3.5) + 3.5$$
$$= 42.875 + 3.5$$
$$= 46.375$$

Lottie says 3.5 is too small, as 46.375 is smaller than 50.

She then tries other numbers to get closer to 50. Here is a summary of her results:

$x =$	$x^3 + x =$	Bigger or smaller than 50?
4	68	Too big
3	30	Too small
3.5	46.375	Too small
3.7	54.353	Too big
3.6	50.256	Too big
3.65	52.277125	Too big
3.55	48.288875	Too small
3.58	49.462712	Too small
3.59	49.858279	Too small
3.595	50.05686988	Too big
3.593	49.97736886	Too small
3.594	50.01710858	Too big
3.5935	49.99723603	Too small
3.5937	50.0051844	Too big

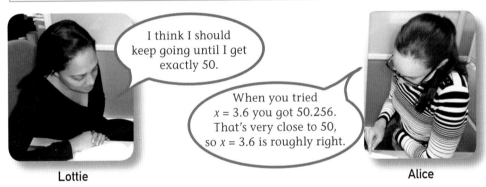

I think I should keep going until I get exactly 50.

When you tried $x = 3.6$ you got 50.256. That's very close to 50, so $x = 3.6$ is roughly right.

Lottie   Alice

What are the advantages and disadvantages of doing what Lottie says and keeping going to try to get exactly 50?

23 What are the advantages and disadvantages of doing what Alice suggests and saying the answer is roughly $x = 3.6$?

24 Alice also says: 'When you were trying numbers you didn't need to try $x = 3.65$.' Look back at the table. Why was it not worth trying $x = 3.65$?

> $x = 3.6$ is the solution of $x^3 + x = 50$ correct to 1 decimal place. In exam questions you are often asked for the solution correct to 1 decimal place (1 d.p.).

25 Carrying on like Lottie wanted to do would get closer to the exact answer but usually 1 decimal place is close enough.

Lottie solves another equation using her 'trial and improvement' method. Here is her working out:

$x =$	$x^2 + 2x =$	Bigger or smaller than 40?
4	$4^2 + (2 \times 4) = 24$	Too small
5	$5^2 + (2 \times 5) = 35$	Too small
6	$6^2 + (2 \times 6) = 48$	Too big
7	$7^2 + (2 \times 7) = 63$	Too big
5.5	$5.5^2 + (2 \times 5.5) = 41.25$	Too big
5.4	$5.4^2 + (2 \times 5.4) = 39.96$	Too small

a) One of Lottie's trials was not needed. Which one and why?

b) Which two whole numbers does the solution lie between?

c) What was the equation that Lottie was solving this time?

d) What is the solution to 1 decimal place?

Student's Book exercise 4.4

1 There is a solution of the equation $x^3 - 4x + 1 = 0$ between 1 and 2. Find a solution correct to 1 decimal place.

2 Show that there is a solution of $x^3 - 5x = 8$ between 2 and 3. Find the solution correct to 1 decimal place.

3 Show that there is a solution of $x^3 - 7x = 25$ between 3 and 4. Find the solution correct to 1 decimal place.

4 Show that there is a solution of $x^2 + 2x - 6 = 0$ between 1 and 2. Find the solution correct to 1 decimal place.

5 Find a solution of $x^3 + x = 15$ correct to 1 decimal place.

6 Find a solution of $x^2 + 3x = 30$ correct to 1 decimal place.

Summary

In this chapter you have seen that there are a variety of ways of solving equations. These include using:

- journeys on a number line
- scales and balancing
- common-sense or EASY TO SEE
- trial and improvement

For some equations you can pick your method. For others you should select the best one.

Class activity 3

Choosing your method

1 Working with a partner, decide how you would solve the following equations using the suggested methods:

   a) $5x + 24 = 3x + 14$ (use the number line and scales and balance)

   b) $2x + 5 = 17$ (use the number line and scales and balance and EASY TO SEE)

   c) $\frac{x}{2} - 3 = 5$ (use the number line and scales and balance and EASY TO SEE)

   d) $4x - 12 = 3x - 7$ (use the number line and scales and balance)

   e) $x^3 + x = 39$ (use trial and improvement)

2 Explain in your own words when you would use each method. (For example, what type of equations are best solved by trial and improvement?)

Back at the chip shop

Fish	£2.60
Sausage	£1.20
Chips	£1.10
Peas	£0.50
Gravy	£0.40

In Chapter 1: At the chip shop, you'll have noticed that Jane and Azim often worked out their orders differently but came to the same answer.

For example Azim wrote down an order as:

$$3(f + c) + 4(s + p) + 1c + 2p + 2(f + p)$$

Jane worked out the cost of this order by writing:

$$5f + 4s + 4c + 8p$$

Explain why they should get the same answer whichever version they use.

2 Write down another way of working out the following orders:

a) $2(f + p) + 5s + 4(f + c) + 3g$

b) $3(f + c + g) + 3(s + g) + 2p + 2c$

3 Azim and Jane are discussng an order of 3 fish, 6 lots of chips and 3 lots of peas.

I do the price of 3 fish, then the price of 6 lots of chips, then the price of 3 lots of peas and add them up.

I do the price of 1 fish, 2 lots of chips and 1 peas, then times that by 3.

To work out the cost of this order, Jane likes to imagine all the food laid out in front of her, while Azim likes to imagine it in bags with the same amount in each bag. So, for the order of 3 fish, 6 lots of chips and 3 lots of peas, Jane would work out: $3f + 6c + 3p$.

While Azim would do: $3(f + 2c + p)$.

a) How many bags is Azim thinking of?

b) What exactly is in each bag?

4 When an order comes in for $4f + 8c + 4g$, Jane tries to help Azim by writing it as $2(2f + 4c + 2g)$.

Azim says, 'I can write it simpler than this by using 4 bags with less in each bag.'

Write down how Azim would have worked out this order.

5 Later on in the day, a customer calls to complain that they have been sent the wrong order. When they ordered over the phone, they asked for '3 lots of fish, chips, and peas'.

a) How would you write down this order?

b) Jane took the order and wrote it as $3f + c + p$. What mistake has Jane made here?

In maths, the way that Jane works out the cost of orders is usually called the **expanded** way. The way that Azim does it is called the **factorised** way.

So, for example, if a customer wants 3 fish and 3 chips:
The **expanded** way of working out the order is $3f + 3c$.
And the **factorised** way of working out the order is $3(f + c)$.

Now turn to pages 23–24 in your workbook and do Workbook exercise 5.1.

6 A customer calls with the following order:

Fish and chips 3 times, please.

3(f + c)

This is what Azim wrote on the order slip:

A few minutes later the customer phoned again and said:

One of my friends is not coming, so could I cancel one fish and one chips.

This is what Azim wrote on the order slip:

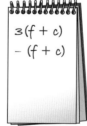

3(f + c)
– (f + c)

How many portions of fish and how many portions of chips will be needed?

7 Another customer calls with the following order:

1 fish and 2 chips, please.

Jane wrote on the order slip:

1f + 2c

The customer then phones back and says:

I forgot my two cousins are coming round, so I need to order an extra two lots of fish and chips.

Jane altered the order slip to:

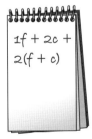

1f + 2c +
2(f + c)

How many portions of fish and how many portions of chips will be needed?

In maths you are sometimes asked to **simplify** an expression. This is similar to the idea of recognising how many portions of each item are needed in the chip shop; like the way Jane works out the cost. So, for example:

$$f + 3c + 3(f + c) + 2p \text{ can be written as}$$
$$f + 3c + 3f + 3c + 2p$$
and then simplified to
$$4f + 6c + 2p.$$

This could also then be factorised (using Azim's way) to $2(2f + 3c + p)$.

In maths we would write:

$$f + 3c + 3(f + c) + 2p = f + 3c + 3f + 3c + 2p$$

$$= 4f + 6c + 2p \qquad \text{(Jane's way)}$$
$$= 2(2f + 3c + p) \qquad \text{(Azim's way)}$$

8 Simplify the following and then try to factorise your answer if possible.

a) $2(f + c) + f + c$

b) $3f + 4s + 2(f + c) + s + 3c$

c) $2f + 3c + 3(s + c) + s$

d) $3(f + c) + 2(s + c) + c + g$

e) $4(f + c) + 3(s + c) + 2(c + g) + 2f + g$

Back to the number line and balance scales

9 In Chapters 2, 3 and 4 of this book you looked at how the balance scales and number line can be used to think about the meaning of expressions with brackets.

a) $3(2x + 4)$ on a number line is:

Say why this must be the same as $6x + 12$.

b) $2(5x + 6) + 3$ on a balance scales is:

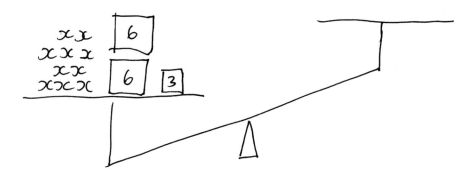

Say why this must be the same as $10x + 15$.

c) $4x + 6y$ on a number line is:

Use the picture above to say why $4x + 6y$ is the same as $2(2x + 3y)$.

d) Draw either a number line diagram or a set of balance scales and use your picture to say why the following must be true:

i) $4(3x + 2) = 12x + 8$

ii) $2(3y + 1) = 6y + 2$

iii) $5(x + 3y) = 5x + 15y$

iv) $6(2a + 3) + 2 = 12a + 20$

v) $3b + 12 = 3(b + 4)$

vi) $4p + 6q = 2(2p + 3q)$

The 'lots of' strategy

Many people use the 'lots of' strategy to expand brackets. They think of it like this:

$3(2x + 4)$ means	3 lots of $(2x + 4)$
which is	$(2x + 4) + (2x + 4) + (2x + 4)$
which is	$6x + 12$
$2(5x + 6) + 3$ means	2 lots of $(5x + 6)$ add another 3
which is	$(5x + 6) + (5x + 6) + 3$
which is	$10x + 12 + 3$
which is	$10x + 15$

$4x + 6y$ can be thought of as 2 lots of $(2x + 3y)$.

10 a) Look at the following expressions and group together the ones which are really the same.

$4(x + y) + 4$ $2(2x + y) + 2(y + 1)$ $2(2x + 2y + 1) + 2$

$2(2x + 2y + 1)$ $x + 3(x + y) + 2$ $3x + 2(y + 1) + (x + y)$

b) Describe the strategies you used to help you decide.

 Now turn to pages 25–26 in your workbook and complete Workbook exercise 5.2.

11 Faiza has been asked to expand $3(2x - 5)$. She says, 'I just think of 3 **lots of** $(2x - 5)$, which gives me $6x - 15$.'

What would Faiza say if she was asked to expand $2(x - 2)$?

12 Gary is trying to factorise $8x - 12$. He says, 'This looks like it has come from 4 **lots of** something.'

a) Why does he say this?   **b)** Factorise $8x - 12$

13 a) Expand the following:

    i) $5(x + 2y)$ **ii)** $3(2x - 5)$ **iii)** $2(3p - 4q)$

    iv) $4(p - 3q - r)$ **v)** $10(a + 3b - 6)$

b) Factorise the following where possible:

    i) $4x - 2y$ **ii)** $6p - 9$ **iii)** $4x + 8y - 10$

    iv) $15a - 4b$ **v)** $20 - 10x - 4y$

14 a) Design 5 expressions similar to the ones in **question 13b)** which can be factorised.

b) Design 5 expressions similar to the ones in **question 13b)** which can not be factorised.

c) Give all 10 expressions to your neighbour for them to try to factorise.

Summary

In this chapter we have looked at how we can write mathematical expressions in different ways.

In maths exams you might be asked to **factorise**, **expand** or **simplify**. These questions are really about being able to write the mathematical statement in a different form.

For example: $3(x + 2y) + 2(2x + 3y) + 2x$

Can be **expanded** to $3x + 6y + 4x + 6y + 2x$

And **simplified** to $9x + 12y$

And **factorised** to $3(3x + 4y)$